Vincent van Gogh was born in Holland in 1853.

His paintings are not the only inheritance he has left us. He has also left us his letters.
To his brother Theo, four years his junior, he confided his innermost thoughts and passions,
feelings that shook him like the wind, as well as his experimentations with color.
After I had read them, I saw the sky, the clouds, and the trees with new eyes,
and I discovered what extraordinary affection can unite two brothers.
— C. L.

Dedicato a chi ci fa stare bene
— C. L.

Alla nostra anima appassionata
— O. M.

Photo Credit:
Originals of Vincent van Gogh © Bridgeman Art Library, London, U.K.

© edizioni ARKA, Milano, 2010

This edition published in 2011 in the United States of America by
Eerdmans Books for Young Readers
An imprint of Wm. B. Eerdmans Publishing Company
2140 Oak Industrial Dr. NE, Grand Rapids, Michigan 49505
P.O. Box 163, Cambridge CB3 9PU U.K.

www.eerdmans.com/youngreaders

17 16 15 14 13 12 11   7 6 5 4 3 2 1

Printed by Stampe Violato, Bagnoli di Sopra, Italy
Bound by LeZana srl, Padua, Italy, July 2010, first printing

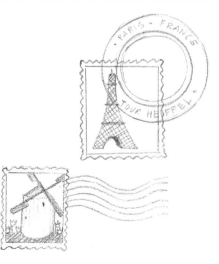

Library of Congress Cataloging-in-Publication Data

Lossani, Chiara.
Vincent van Gogh and the colors of the wind / by Chiara Lossani ; illustrated by Octavia Monaco.
p. cm.
ISBN 978-0-8028-5390-5 (alk. paper)
1. Gogh, Vincent van, 1853–1890 — Juvenile literature. 2. Painters — Netherlands — Biography — Juvenile literature.
I. Gogh, Vincent van, 1853–1890. II. Monaco, Octavia. III. Title.
ND653.G7L67 2011
759.9492 — dc22
[B]
                    2010028330

Vincent van Gogh
and the Colors of the Wind

Text by Chiara Lossani
inspired by the artist's letters to Theo

Illustrations by Octavia Monaco

Eerdmans Books for Young Readers
Grand Rapids, Michigan • Cambridge, U.K.

Spring has painted a blanket of flowers in the fields surrounding the parish house where the Van Gogh family lives, in Zundert.

Vincent is running, his mouth open wide, as if to swallow the wind.

"Theo, come! It's beautiful!" he cries out to his younger brother.

The wind ruffles their red hair, joining these two brothers,

so alike and yet so different, in a single embrace.

Vincent observes the spiders among the blades of grass. Theo observes them too.

Vincent leafs through his uncle's art books. Theo does the same.

Vincent draws everything his eye falls on. Theo draws too.

"Your drawings are better than mine, though," Theo admits with a smile.

And yet, Theo walks, while Vincent runs.

Theo speaks in a composed manner, while Vincent gestures wildly, like a windmill.

Theo plays with everyone, while Vincent quarrels with everyone.

That's why all their friends include Theo in their games, but shun Vincent.

But Theo would do anything for his brother.

He would run through the fields until his heart burst.

You'll always be close, murmurs the wind,

even when I blow different destinies your way.

When Vincent turns sixteen, he leaves the family home. Theo leaves soon after.
An uncle finds them both jobs in various art galleries, in The Hague, in Paris,
in London — but never together in the same city.
Vincent is happy, immersed in this new world.
He writes enthusiastically to his brother, "Painters teach us to see."

For now, he can only draw. In the corners, in the margins, and at the foot of his letters,
words become lost in a sea of landscapes, trees, and churches.

However, Vincent doesn't enjoy every part of his work.
How are things going with the customers? murmurs the wind one day.
He just shrugs. "They fired me. I argued with everyone.
I can't stand having to sell ugly pictures, pretending they are beautiful!"
And with the girls . . . ?
Vincent shakes his head, his heart bleeding. "The girls reject me, they make me suffer."
Vincent is no longer happy. He feels let down by everyone, lost. His thoughts burn
through his mind, and only prayer and the Bible give him some comfort.

What do you want to do, Vincent? Don't you have a dream? howls the wind.
Yes, a dream makes its timid appearance in Vincent's mind:
"I'd like to become a preacher, like my father,
and take the light of the Gospels to the poor."
Go, go! Leave everything behind, change your life! howls the wind.

Vincent hurls himself headlong into his theological studies. Day and night, he buries his head in the Gospels, while his hand fills the margins of his copybooks with drawings. Then one day his dream comes true. He is sent to Belgium, to preach in the coal mines. He shares everything with the miners: he gives all he's got; he takes care of them when they are ill; he descends into the mines and speaks to them about painting. He gives and gives until he wears himself out.

"This life is too hard for you, Vincent!" Theo worries in his letters.

Don't listen to him, says the wind.

"You don't eat, you don't sleep, you live in the dark," writes Theo.

Art, too, can bring light, says the wind.

It's true. Under a smoke-burdened sky, few of the sun's rays reach the earth's surface, while miserable huts and enormous piles of coal make for a very desolate landscape.

And yet, Vincent's eyes pick out positive images:

"Thornbushes rise like charcoal sketches, while the miners returning to their huts look like soot-covered chimney sweeps," he writes.

"Please, find a less strenuous job!" begs Theo.

No, Vincent won't listen.

The two brothers argue. The letters stop.

Even Vincent's superiors scold him.

"How can you be a good preacher if you dress in rags and talk about Jesus and paintings with the same passion?" they ask, as they fire him.

The wind howls out in Vincent's mind.

What will you do next? What will you become?

Vincent has failed.
Far from home and out of work, having lost Theo's friendship,
he feels trapped, enveloped in the darkness of his thoughts like a bird in a cage.
He knows there is good inside him, but what is it exactly?
Why can't he find it?

The wind caresses his hair, blowing away these dark thoughts one by one,
like molting feathers. *Do not be afraid of changing again,* it says.
Open your heart. Start to paint what you see and feel!
Try imitating the great masters you have admired in the museums.

A new dream boldly makes its way in his mind.
Vincent feels that painting may be his answer to the world.
The silence between the two brothers finally breaks.
"Loving one another breaks open the prison doors!" he writes. "I'll be a painter!"

Theo instantly opens his loving arms
and sends Vincent money from Paris
for the rent, for food, for paints and canvases.

"Think only of painting, my brother.
I'll sell your pictures!" he writes.

Vincent's life is bathed in a new light.
A fresh adventure is about to start.

Music and harmony ring in Vincent's heart.

He draws by day and reads painting technique books by night.
At times, he attends lessons held by artist friends, but Nature is his true teacher.
It is she who teaches him about light, shapes, and shadows.
Under her guidance, even the barest trees and the most miserable huts
become painting subjects.

"Who's that madman dressed like a scarecrow wandering in the fields with canvases
under one arm and paintbrushes under the other?" murmur the crowds.
Vincent ignores them. "They treat me like a dog
with wet paws that no one wants to let into their home,
but I don't care. I'll teach them what lies
in the heart of this madman through my paintings!"

But how difficult to depict on canvas what one sees and feels!

At first, the paintbrush sits rigidly between Vincent's fingers, but then,
after numerous drawings, watercolors, and oil paintings, it becomes flexible.
And now his canvases begin to depict fields and huts, peasants using their hands
to dig the earth, using their hands to eat potatoes.

"What sets a valuable painting apart from the rest?" writes Theo.
"The masters' paintings contain a precious gem, the human soul. I too want to find
my way into people's hearts," replies Vincent. His eyes rest on the many canvases
that fill his studio: dark landscapes in which he has re-created human misery,
hard labor, and suffering, in somber, earthy colors.

In Paris, however, no one likes those dark paintings.

You need bright colors, Vincent.
But Holland is the wrong place for those, murmurs the wind.
Go to Paris, to Theo, and watch how the Impressionists work.

In Paris, in Père Tanguy's workshop, Vincent discovers paintings full of color and light.
The old salesman loves the Impressionists' work and is a friend of Pissarro,
Toulouse-Lautrec, Seurat, and Gauguin, who visit him day after day
to discuss their style of painting.
Vincent observes them, admires them, and gets caught up in their wind:
a passion for colors and sensations.

After some time, Père Tanguy displays Vincent's latest paintings.
They are very different from those he painted in Holland;
he has discovered color in the world around him.
The roofs of Paris, the windmills of Montmartre, the trees, the terraces,
and the gardens are all full of blues and greens.
The flowers are red poppies, yellow chrysanthemums, white and pink roses.

This is a happy time for Vincent: he lives with Theo and has lots of friends.
Time with them passes by quickly, discussing painting,
dreaming of a shared home in which to paint freely,
painting each others' portraits,
exhibiting paintings in cafés,
and, yes, sometimes quarreling.
But in time, these disputes transform increasingly into brawls,
and the parties become rowdy.
Theo begins to find it difficult to live with Vincent
as he grows more insufferable day by day —
perhaps the alcohol he has started drinking doesn't help?
Theo is worried.
A painter friend tells him, "Yesterday, during an argument
at Père Tanguy's, Vincent was so enraged
that he stripped naked in front of everyone."

That evening Theo says to his brother,
"For you, life in the city is like wearing
an outfit that's too tight."

Even the wind says,
That's enough! There's no peace to be found in Paris.
You simply can't work this way!
And so the wind drives Vincent away, toward silence, toward bright skies.

Sun! Light! Yellow! In Arles, in the south of France, even dreams are colorful.
Vincent makes peace with himself and with his Parisian friends.
Look at that yellow house, Vincent! There is your shared home! murmurs the wind.
Vincent rents the house, and even though at first he sleeps on the floor
and has only a table for furniture, he imagines it full of art and happiness.
He soon furnishes it with wide, square furniture, a yellow bed, and lots of paintings.

At night he dreams, while during the day . . . ah, during the day he plunges into the light!
Surrounded by nature, he brushes aside all he has learned in Paris.
He observes colors and invents new ones: the purple of olives for the shadows
of the groves, the silvery pink for the sea, the warm tones of bread crusts for wheat.

The wind encourages him:
Paint that field. Look at it well, Vincent. It is an ocean of sunlight!
The brushstrokes follow one another, and the colors chase each other like words
in a speech, while golden ears of wheat appear on the canvas.
The sunflowers, Vincent! The sheaves! The sun!
Vincent squeezes tubes of paint onto his canvases. His sun is so bright
that even sunset is unable to quench it. His sheaves are mounds of gold.

Every day, Vincent rides the wind,
treading through the fields with his easel on his back.

The wind in Provence is called the Mistral.
It howls and fills the canvases like sails on the sea.
At times it is mischievous.
"Blasted wind!" cries Vincent, chasing sheets of paper
that the wind spitefully carries off.

As soon as Vincent has found a suitable spot,
the Mistral blows his easel away.
And so Vincent anchors it to the ground with pegs and rope.
It won't be the wind that'll stop him from painting . . .

Nor the darkness.
At sunset, Vincent steps out wearing a straw hat on which he has strapped some candles.
"I want to paint the night . . ."
With that hat? You must be mad! cries the wind.
"The streets, the brightly lit cafés, and . . ." Vincent lifts his eyes, "above all, the sky!"
Didn't he write one day to Theo, "I yearn for the stars I cannot reach"?
But if he can't reach them physically, at least he can now try through his paintings!
And so, as the stars glimmer brightly in shades of green, yellow, white, and light blue,
on Vincent's canvases they become emeralds, opals, diamonds, and sapphires.

But in the cafés, frequented by drunks, Vincent feels like he's in hell.
That's why he paints their walls the color of wine, and the gas lamps
like sulphur yellow eyes. Sulphur yellow is also the color of the face
he paints for Patience, the peasant who sits dejectedly at his tableside night after night.
The colors are absolute, solid, without nuances.
They express the invisible: people and objects as Vincent *feels* them.
They tell of another reality, of a night time
which exists elsewhere . . .

In Paris, these paintings leave Theo flabbergasted.

Gauguin, too, is thunderstruck.

And he finally decides to go to Arles, where Vincent had long been waiting for him.

Now, the two friends live together in the yellow house.

The sun bathes the pictures hanging on the walls in a golden light.

Gauguin can almost smell the perfume of the sunflowers Vincent has painted for him.

Caught up in the frenzy of painting and seeking new colors, at first they get along.

But then?

Can two volcanoes stand side by side without causing a calamity?

"You're too untidy," Gauguin scolds Vincent, picking up newly opened

and freshly squeezed tubes of paint all over the floor.

"You throw away money without a thought!"

"While you work with half a heart, Paul! Half of it is here, and the other half in Paris!"

In time, the first moments of joy are burned up. Tussles follow, along with heavy accusations and nasty looks. Vincent becomes gloomy. Once, waking up in the middle of the night, Gauguin finds Vincent standing at the foot of his bed, staring at him with cold eyes, a razor in his hand. Gauguin can't take any more. He returns to Paris.

Desperate, in a moment of anguish, Vincent cuts his own ear.
"What has he done? Has he gone mad?" whisper the neighbors.
A doctor has him hospitalized.

When he returns home, Vincent finds the house empty.
Sadness.
Solitude.
He paints Gauguin's chair: elegant, with a book and a candle.
He paints his own: simple, with a pipe and some tobacco.
Neither is occupied.
Where is the friend with whom he hoped to conquer the world with colors?
And his old dreams — where have they gone?
Vincent is unwell. His mind is unwell.
When lucidity returns, he looks at himself in the mirror.
Does he paint himself with a bandage so that he won't forget his injured ear?

A moment of anguish is followed by another, and then another . . .
Vincent can no longer live alone. He prefers to go to a hospital, and writes to Theo,
"I'm at the hospital in Saint Remy. Here I feel safe. They can treat me.
The surrounding landscape is so beautiful,
and the garden is dotted with purple irises and tufts of lilac.
Pity about that blasted Mistral, which howls so!"
Vincent chases it with his eyes, his paintbrush and palette in hand.
Catch me if you can! I'm here, on the tip of the cypress! howls the wind.
"Caught you!"
I'm here, among the olive trees.
"Caught you!"
Here, making waves with the poppies and wheat. Look up: I'm in the clouds.
Look at me dance with the stars and the moon! Look down: I'm in the bushes!
I'm in the grass! And further still: see how I can even make the mountains move?
That blasted Mistral would drive you mad!
But Vincent can always catch it.
His canvases fill with color.
And wind.

His anguish goes, and comes back, and then goes again, like the wind.
Now Vincent would like to leave the hospital and go and live near his brother.
Theo agrees. He will take him to Dr. Gachet.

Dr. Gachet lives close to Paris, in Auvers.
He is a friend of the painters. He has promised to cure Vincent.
Vincent goes to see him every day. They often talk about painting.
"Theo has sold one of your paintings in Paris!" the doctor announces one day.
Vincent nods, with fatigue. "Someone has started to appreciate my work."
How many paintings does a painter have to sell to live comfortably?
A thousand? Three thousand? He has painted seven hundred,
but he has sold only one.
"How are you today?" asks Dr. Gachet.
Vincent shows him the sheaves of wheat he has just painted.
"They look like flames, Vincent."
"The same goes for the thoughts in my head."

In Auvers, in July, the sky is always ready to break into a storm.
Vincent has quarreled with Dr. Gachet, too. He feels even more lonely, more gloomy.
He is painting a picture. He describes it to Theo:
"Expanses of wheat under tormented skies . . .
I had no difficulty expressing my sadness, my extreme solitude."

He has almost finished it. It may even be finished today. He returns to the wheat field.
He lifts his eyes to the sky and seeks out the wind
that is pulling the clouds about like heavy chains.
One hand, in his pocket, brushes against the cold metal of a gun.
The other starts to paint.
The ears of wheat break under the wind and the brushstrokes.
A flock of crows caws in the distance. It moves closer.
Vincent follows its flight with his gaze.
He invites it onto the canvas.

The beating of wings fills the space, suffocating it.

A shot rings out in the air.
The paintbrush falls to the ground.
The crows fly away, frightened.

In the evening, Vincent returns home, injured.

The next day Theo races to Auvers.
There is little time left for the two brothers to reminisce.
During the night, Vincent dies.
It is the 29th of July, 1890.
Vincent is only thirty-seven years old.

His friends lay sunflowers on his grave.

In Paris, a feeling of sorrow takes hold of Theo.
"Oh, Vincent, all that is left of you are your paintings . . .
And I had just started selling them."

Through the half-open window, a gust of wind throws the panes wide open,
draws the flame of the candle toward the canvases, and makes the colors tremble.
The sunflowers sway, the stars flicker,
the ears of wheat and the tips of the cypresses bend.
You'll always be close . . . murmurs the wind.
Then, with a last cold blast, it blows out the candle.

Theo dies on the 28th of January, 1891, six months after Vincent.

TRADITIONAL
HOME BOOK OF
H·E·R·B·S

MICHAEL JANULEWICZ

TODTRI

DEDICATION

For Juliana

This book was designed and produced by
Todtri Productions Limited
P.O. Box 572
New York, NY 10116-0572
Fax (212) 279-1241

Printed and bound in Singapore

ISBN 1-880908-40-9

Author: Michael Janulewicz

Publisher: Robert M. Tod
Designer and Art Director: Ron Pickless
Editor: Nicolas Wright
Typeset and DTP: Blanc Verso/UK

CONTENTS

INTRODUCTION

Talk of perfect happiness or pleasure, and what
place was so fit for that as the garden place where
Adam was set to be a herbalist.
GERARD

Every garden brings its own delight to its gardener, usually
in equal measure to frustration, and disappointment too.
Herb gardening is no different, but personally more
rewarding than growing prize roses or chrysanthemums.
This book is about herbs more than gardening, and I trust this
will not disappoint too much. I hope that the seasoned
gardener will find new ideas and new things to try, but equally
that the new gardener will discover the joy of growing
herbs for their own sake.
There are many facets to the fascination of herbs - first, they are
useful in so many ways, from food to cosmetics and medicines,
but they are also a living link with human history. The fact
that most garden herbs are little changed from the wild species
and have been collected and cultivated for thousands of years,
means that this link is continuous and direct. The very names
conjure up a past that we can only otherwise capture in books
and the nature of the often fanciful claims to the efficacy of herbs
plunges us into a magical world before the scientific age.
The motto of the American Herb Society adequately sums up
what herbs are to today's gardener - 'For use and delight'. And
both come true with a little care and effort.

Michael Janulewicz

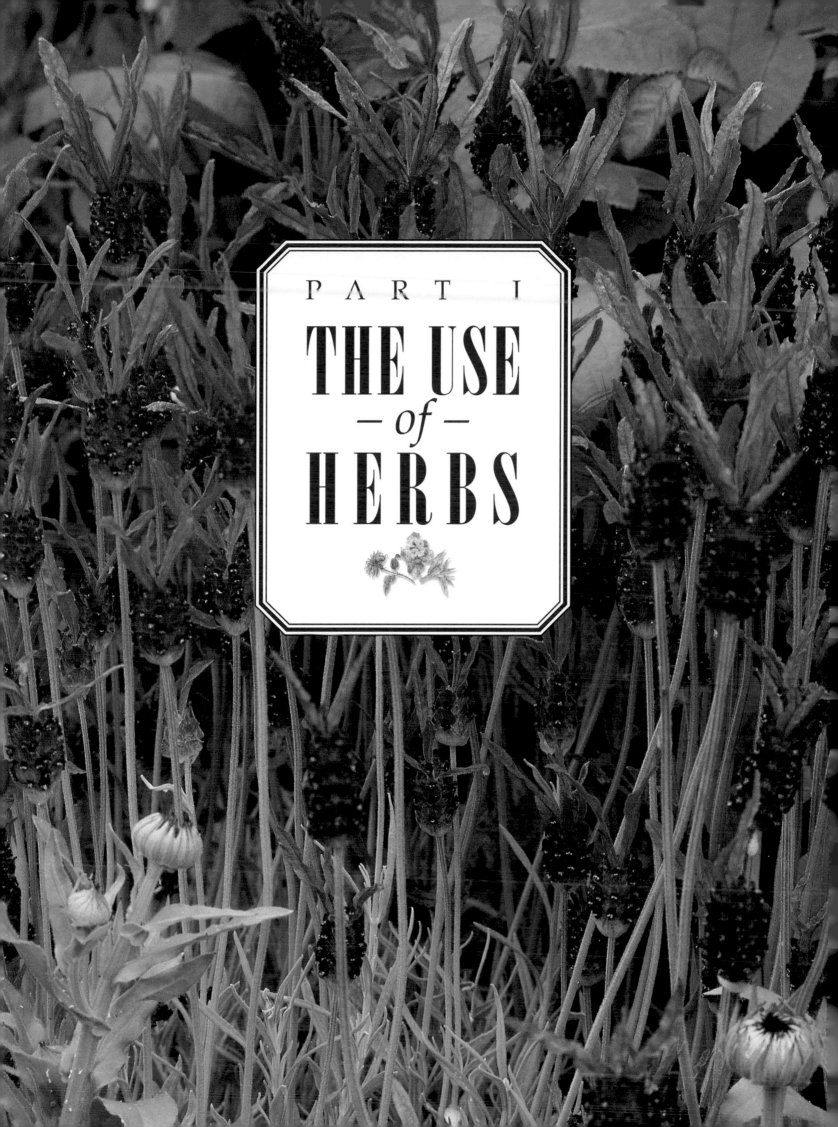

PART I

THE USE
_— of —_
HERBS

A SHORT HISTORY OF HERB GARDENING

Above: 'Six bunches a penny, sweet blooming Lavender' was one of the historic cries of the street traders of London. All kinds of herbs were brought from the country to be sold in street markets up until World War II.

Opposite: The Chelsea Physic Garden, London, England: Founded by the Society of Apothecaries in 1673, the Chelsea garden remained in the hands of the apothecaries until the turn of the century and is little changed. The herbs are grouped according to their uses for example culinary, medicinal and dyeing.

With no written records of early human societies we cannot be sure when plants were first cultivated in what we would recognize today as a garden. Archaeological evidence, however, does show that early humans relied on plants for clothing, food and medicine and it is probably safe to assume that the most valued plants were transplanted from the wild to be cultivated closer to the protection of home.

The first written records appear in Egypt, Assyria and China and the fragmentary evidence shows that plants were extensively used as medicines with well over two hundred drugs being prescribed. With the flowering of the Classical Age in Ancient Greece and Rome we find extensive records from 300 BC to the latter half of the first century when Pliny the Elder listed more than a thousand plants in his work *Historia naturalis.*

The Romans introduced plants to, and collected them from, every corner of their Empire. Yet still there is no evidence that the plants were ever regarded as anything more than useful, and ornamental gardening, as opposed to raising crops, probably did not exist in a formal manner, other than in the houses of noblemen. With the fall of the Roman Empire many of the conquered lands returned to their local folk beliefs in plants, but within the Christian monasteries of Europe the more scientific tradition was upheld, with gardens full of medicinal and food plants laid out within the grounds.

Meanwhile, the Islamic encroachment through North Africa and eventually into Spain by the seventh century saw Arab scholars continuing the Greek tradition and discipline of science.

The importance of plants to sustain communities was never lost. At the coronation of Charlemagne, leader of the Holy Roman Empire, in 800, it was decreed that a list of eighty-nine plants should be grown in every city. But still the understanding of plants and medicine was based on the Greek and Roman orthodoxy until the European Renaissance of the seventeenth century.

In 1439 there was one event that changed the world. When Johannes Gutenberg developed movable type and the printing press, information about the world was suddenly available to

Above: A tempting display of culinary herbs in a French market garden.

more people, more quickly and more cheaply. Although the Bible was the first printed book, a collection of Herbals soon followed and we owe virtually all of our historic knowledge of gardening to these early editions, although most were still based on translations — often very bad translations — of the original Greek texts.

With the discovery of the Americas more and more plant material was available and the traffic in plant stock and seeds was regarded as of prime importance and a potential source of wealth and power. Potatoes, tomatoes and tobacco were some of the earliest imports and now regarded as almost natives. Yet at the same time the first formal gardens were being laid out, mostly geometric patterns of hedges of such plants as box, thyme and cotton lavender. These were filled in with plants to complete the pattern - a style that reached the height of its popularity in Elizabethan knot gardens, its zenith in the great parterres of Versailles and its nemesis in Victorian carpet bedding, unfortunately still practised by town and city landscapers today.

Opposite: Plimouth Plantation, MA: The reconstructed houses and gardens of the early colonial period show how herbs were grown in raised-bed kitchen gardens.